Dudley M. Canright

Matter and Spirit

Dudley M. Canright

Matter and Spirit

ISBN/EAN: 9783337118525

Printed in Europe, USA, Canada, Australia, Japan

Cover: Foto ©Lupo / pixelio.de

More available books at **www.hansebooks.com**

MATTER AND SPIRIT;

PROBLEM OF HUMAN THOUGHT.

A PHILOSOPHICAL ARGUMENT.

BY ELDER D. M. CANRIGHT.

"I will praise Thee; for I am fearfully and wonderfully made."
—*Psalmist.*

BATTLE CREEK, MICH.:
REVIEW & HERALD PUBLISHING HOUSE.
1882.

PUBLISHERS' NOTE.

THE subject treated in this work is intimately
connected with many of the problems that are being freely discussed in the religious world at the
present day. The publishers believe that the
plain and logical method with which the author
has dealt with the question will greatly assist the
reader in the solution of these problems, and di-
vest them of many of their intricacies by estab-
lishing correct premises upon which to base conclusions. Commending it to the careful consider-
ation of the candid reader, they send it forth on
its mission, asking the blessing of Heaven on its
perusal.

CONTENTS

MATTER AND SPIRIT;

OR THE

Problem of Human Thought.

―――◄•►―――

INTRODUCTORY.

IS anything too hard for God? Is he not almighty? Certain persons limit the power of God when they claim that matter cannot be organized by the Almighty so as to be able to think and reason. They take up a stone, they weigh it, measure it, and divide it, and then ask if that thing can think. Of course not. Examine that piece of wood. Can it think? Take a handful of the dust of the ground, from which all things grow. Is there anything here able to think? They analyze a dead body, and find that it is made up chiefly of water, nitrogen, a little phosphorus, a little sulphur, and some lime, with a few other earthy materials. Go farther, and analyze a man's brain. It is found to be composed of eight-tenths water, with a little albumen, a little fat, phosphorus, sulphur, etc. Then they ask us if these

(7)

elements can think. Can sulphur reason? Can
water love? Can oxygen hate? No. Hence they
conclude that no matter, in whatever form or organization, can be made to think. And, therefore,
all intelligences, whether men, angels, or Deity,
must be immaterial. So heaven is fancied to be
a vast region entirely void of matter. God who
dwells there has no body, no form, no visible
parts, but is a mere essence pervading all space.
The angels are the same in essence, having no
bodies, being nothing that can be felt, or handled,
or seen. The souls of men are the same also in
kind,—bodiless, intangible essences. All matter
is incapable of thought, and all intelligence pro-
ceeds from immateriality. One more assumption,
and the hard labored conclusion is triumphantly
reached; namely, Whatever is immaterial is indestructible and therefore immortal. Hence the
thinking part of man is immortal.

But let us examine this pretentious fabric. If
God is without body, parts, or shape, a mere essence filling all space, and if angels and the souls
of men are the same, only smaller, then how can
either be a person, or have a separate existence
from the other? But waiving this, where is the
proof that an immaterial being cannot be destroyed? Has God said so? No. Do they know
it by experience? No. Then it is a mere ground-
less assumption. This theory of the immateriality of the soul is a modern invention to sustain

the tottering notion of the soul's immortality. But the most noted theologians now confess that immateriality does not prove immortality. That which had a beginning can have an end. What God has made, he can destroy.

But to the question, Can God organize matter so that it can think? we answer, Yes. But our opponents say, "A stone, a stick, dust, water, iron,—these are material. They have no intelligence. Hence matter cannot think." True, matter in these particular forms cannot think; but it does not follow that it cannot in a different form, or when differently organized. A ball of snow is very white and very cold. It is material. Shall I therefore conclude that all matter must be white and cold? A piece of coal is just as material as the snow-ball; and yet it is very black, just opposite in color from the snow. Again, burning coal is very hot, just the opposite of the cold snow. Has it ceased to be material? Lift that block of lead. How very heavy! Now handle those feathers. How light! They seem to be just the opposite of each other, yet both are matter. One form of matter is sour, as a lemon; another is sweet, as sugar.

Indeed, the various combinations of matter may be said to be almost infinite. Yet it takes only a very few original or primary elements to make all these. "The number of the elements, or simple substances, with which we are at present

acquainted, is sixty-four. These substances are
not all equally distributed over the surface of the
earth: most of them are exceedingly rare, and
only known to chemists. Some ten or twelve
only make up the great bulk, or mass, of all
the objects we see around us." * But God has so
variously arranged and organized these few elements that many forms seem the very opposite
of others, as we have mentioned; as heat and
cold, black and white, light and heavy, sour and
sweet, and yet all are material.

ORGANIZATION OF MATTER IMPARTS TO IT NEW QUALITIES.

It is objected that no combination or organization of material particles can give to matter any
new qualities it did not possess before. But nature
furnishes a thousand illustrations contradicting
this statement. One of the characteristic properties of steam is its remarkable elasticity; but
when it is condensed into water, this property of
the matter entirely disappears, and is replaced by
an exactly opposite property called incompressibil-
ity. So hardness and brilliancy are distinctive
properties of the diamond, yet both these totally
disappear when the gem is converted into a gas,
though not a particle of the matter is lost. So a

* Wells' Natural Philosophy, pp. 11, 12.

cold piece of steel is hard and brittle, but when heated, is soft and ductile. Here is a cold lump of lime. I pour upon it a quantity of cold water, and immediately both become extremely hot. Who has not seen two colorless liquids when poured together become of a bright color, as red or pink? A candle is burning in a room. I blow out the blaze, and all is total darkness. Have I destroyed a particle of that matter? No; yet I have destroyed the light which was a property of that matter in that condition. A change of condition in matter, then, does change its properties. So it is reasonable that by the organization of particles in the brain, thought may be produced when none of those particles separately could think.

I hold in my hand two kernels of corn exactly alike. I plant one, and it has the property of appropriating to itself the particles of matter which surround it, and of building up a stalk of corn. The other kernel I break up fine, and carefully bury every particle of it together. Can it sprout? Can it grow? Will it now build up a stalk? No, indeed. Why? Simply because I have broken up the peculiar arrangement of its particles which gave it the property to do that. The particles are all there, but differently arranged. In crushing that kernel to meal did I drive out a living, immaterial spirit entity which now goes off to live somewhere else? No one claims such a thing. Organization, then, does give to matter qualities which it does not possess unorganized. Now take a higher organization,—a living man. He is thinking. A timber falls and crushes him to death. Can he think or reason now? No, and why not? That organization which gave him this attribute is destroyed, and hence thought ceases.

We utterly deny the distinction between matter and spirit which is claimed. We believe that everything is material, and that these diversities previously mentioned are only different conditions of matter. No man can successfully deny this. The wisest and most scientific men freely admit that they know but little about matter. The more they study, and the deeper they search into it, the more they are convinced that its different attributes and capabilities have been but partially understood. Because a certain fact is true of matter in one condition, it is argued that it must be true of matter always and everywhere. But this is illogical and false, for matter is capable of infinite diversity. Matter in one form may even seem to be the opposite of the same matter in another form. For instance, I have before me a piece of ice. I put my hand upon it; it is exceedingly cold. It is a square block; I can cut it with a knife, or saw it with a saw into blocks. It is solid. But I put this ice into a vessel and warm it. It soon becomes water,—a liquid. It now looks very different from that piece of ice which I held in my hand a few minutes before. I closely confine this water in a tight vessel, and heat it very hot. It now becomes steam, a vapor, and is invisible. Says Mr. Wells, "Steam, which is the vapor of boiling water, is invisible, but when it comes in contact with air, which is cooler, it becomes condensed into small drops, and is thus rendered visible."* It is so hot it would scald your hand in a moment. It can neither be cut, nor poured from vessel to vessel. It now seems to be precisely the opposite from that piece of ice, and yet it is the very same material, only in another condition.

If a man had never seen ice thus converted into steam, he would pronounce such a change impossible. Let him examine a piece of ice, put his hands upon it, and then let him examine steam in its most heated condition; let him try it with his hand, then tell him that they are both the same material, and he would pronounce it the greatest absurdity imaginable. Yet we all know by actual observation that ice, and water, and steam are only different conditions of the same material.

There is apparently as great a difference between steam and ice as is claimed by our opponents between spirit and matter. We claim, therefore, that they cannot show that a spirit is not one form of matter. The Bible nowhere says

* Wells' Natural Philosophy, p. 238.

it is not.   On the other hand, it plainly shows
that it is.

So because matter in one form does not reason,
it is no evidence that it cannot when organized in
some other way.   Look at that coarse, filthy mud
in the road.   That is matter.   Shall we conclude
that all matter is like that?   How absurd! for
here lies a beautiful gold watch, measuring off the
seconds, minutes, and hours in exact time!   The
watch is as material as the mud, but how different!   Again, there is a piece of black charcoal,
hardly worth picking up.   Here is a diamond of
priceless value, one as large as a thimble being
worth millions.   Two small diamond ear-rings
sold for $75,000.   One diamond owned by Napo-
leon was worth $1,000,000.   The king of Portugal
has one worth $28,000,000.   Now, that charcoal
and that diamond are not only both material; but,
wonderful to tell, they are both of exactly the
same material, only differently arranged.   The
contrast between senseless matter and thinking
matter would not be greater.

CONFESSIONS OF EMINENT MEN.

How presumptuous for puny man, with his
narrow range of vision and almost utter ignorance
of the ways and means of the Almighty, and the
endless capabilities of matter, to say what God

can do with matter and what he cannot do! Though for six thousand years men have been using matter, handling matter, eating it, drinking it, wearing it, surrounded on every side by matter, and they themselves are made of it; yet how little do they know about it!

The most profound philosophers, the keenest students of nature, the sharpest chemists, acknowledge their ignorance of the simplest forms and operations of matter. Bishop Clark makes this confession: "If it is asked what is meant by matter, or what matter *is*, we must confess that we know not what constitutes its *essence*. In this respect its ontology is beyond our reach; and the only advance we find it possible to make is to point out *some* of the properties of matter as discerned by our senses, and to exhibit *some* of the laws by which it is governed." *

Yes, all that the wisest man can do is to tell a few of the laws and properties of matter. Here they are stranded on the shore. The great ocean lies beyond them, all unknown. So said Sir Isaac Newton, the prince of philosophers. Another learned author says: "All the great forces or agents in nature, those which produce, or are the cause of, all the changes which take place in matter, may be enumerated as follows: Internal, or molecular forces, the attraction of gravitation, heat, light, the attractive and repulsive forces of

* Man All Immortal, p. 21.

magnetism and electricity, and finally, a force or power which only exists in living animals and plants, which is called *vital force.* Concerning the real nature of these forces, we are entirely ignorant. . . . . . In the present state of science, it is impossible to know whether they are merely properties of matter, or whether they are forms of matter itself."* When scientific men make such confessions of their ignorance of matter, others would better be more modest in their statements.

All confess that they know as little about what spirit is as about what matter is. Here is what a believer in immaterialism says, "Now we are frank to confess that we do not know precisely what a spiritual body is. Some of its characteristics may be, perhaps, pretty well defined, and that is about as far as we can go."† A doctor of divinity says, "It must *not* be thought amiss, nor awaken surprise, if we confess that we know not in what the essence of soul, or spirit, consists."‡ They can neither tell what matter is nor what spirit is, so they are all compelled to confess. Then how do they know that spirit is not one form of matter? Is not the spirit located in the body? Certainly. Well, whatever has locality must have extension, must have a center and circumference, and hence must be material.

* Wells' Natural Philosophy, p. 21.
† N. V. Hull, Editor *Sabbath Recorder,* Aug. 30, 1877.
‡ Man All Immortal, p. 29.

Newham writes: "We do not consider the question of the materiality of the soul as being very important, because what we call spiritual may, in fact, be an infinitely fine modification of matter, far too subtile to be apprehended by our present powers." *

Dr. Knapp says: "This doctrine respecting the immateriality of the soul, in the strict philosophical sense of the term, is of far less consequence to their religion than is commonly supposed. The reason why so much importance has been supposed to be attached to this doctrine is, it was considered as essential to the metaphysical proof of the immortality of the soul. But since the immateriality of the soul, in the strictest sense, can never be made fully and obviously certain, whatever philosophical arguments may be urged in its favor, the proof of immortality should not be built upon it. †

To these pertinent testimonies we add one more, that of the renowned philosopher, John Locke, who says: "We have the ideas of matter and thinking, but possibly shall never be able to know whether any mere material being thinks or not; it being impossible for us, by the contemplation of our own ideas, without revelation, to discover whether Omnipotence has not given to some systems of matter, fitly disposed, a power to per-

* Body and Mind, p. 97.
† Christian Theology, Vol. ii, p. 372.

ceive and think, or else joined and fixed to matter
so disposed, a thinking, immaterial substance; it
being, in respect of our notions, not much more re-
mote from our comprehension to conceive that God
can, if he pleases, superadd to matter a faculty of
thinking, than that he should superadd to it another substance, with a faculty of thinking; since
we know not wherein thinking consists, nor to
what sort of substance the Almighty has been
pleased to give that power which cannot be in
any created being but merely by the good pleas-
ure of the Creator. For I see no contradiction in
it, that the first eternal thinking Being should, if
he pleased, give to certain systems of created,
senseless matter, put together as he thinks fit,
some degrees of sense, perception, and thought." *
Then, for all that the wisest men can tell, it may
be matter after all which thinks.

WHAT IS MATTER?

Who can tell what light is? You are in a
dark room. You hold in your hand a match.
It is nothing but a bit of wood and a little phosphorus,—both gross matter, and no light in either
of them. You scratch the match, and lo! the
whole room is full of light. What is that light?
It is not a living thing, an immaterial intelligence,

* Essay, Book iv., chap. 3.

is it? No; it must be matter in some form, or some action of matter. But why does it give light? We see that it does, but it is hard to tell why. Is not the production of light out of these dark materials in the above case as wonderful as the production of thought by the human, material brain? The one is as inexplicable as the other. Light travels with the velocity of 180,000 miles a second, that is, seven times around the earth while you are winking your eye once! Yet this same light is either material or some action of matter; for it can be analyzed. Pass a ray of light through a prism, and it is separated into seven distinct parts; *viz.*, red, orange, yellow, green, blue, indigo, and violet.* Can the body of an angel be of a purer or higher substance than this? It may be; for perhaps God has matter in his great laboratory far more refined than any with which we have to do.

"As there are forces in the universe unknown and even inconceivable to man, so there may also be celestial bodies called spirits totally unlike what he sees about him, real and substantial each in its kind, but too subtile for human understanding. Science asserts that there is no such thing as pure space. The air is displaced by our walking through it, and the ether may be cut in twain by an angel's winged form, our eyes perceiving neither air, ether, nor angel. Man's ignorance of

* Wells' Natural Philosophy, p. 326.

the essence of things is too patent. Spirits, good
and bad, belong to the realm of the supernatural,
are of the order of the celestial material, but not
gross. I think God may have some other substances besides 'oxygen, nitrogen, and carbon' out
of which to make them. Science, very probably,
could neither 'weigh, analyze, nor measure' Ga-
briel. Nevertheless, this royal being is somebody,
and immateriality, as referred to him and his
heavenly fellows, is a misnomer, a theological
blunder." *

But it is not necessary to suppose any other
substances than those with which we are already
acquainted. A being created out of light, electricity, air, and heat would be sufficiently elevated to meet our highest conceptions of even a
seraph. What is heat? I enter a cold room.
The stove is cold, the wood is cold, the match is
cold. I light the match, ignite the wood, and
shortly the room is filled with heat. What is
that? From whence did it come? It is produced
by gross matter and nothing else. We can feel
it, we can see the effects of it; but here our
knowledge stops. Neither heat nor light has any
weight. Take the most powerful burning-glass,
and pour ten thousand rays of light upon the
most delicate balance, and they will have no per-
ceptible weight. So an iron rod as cold as ice, or

* D. T. Taylor, in *Bible Banner.*

white hot does not vary a particle in weight.* What are they then? Not immaterial, intelligent spirits certainly. They are either a subtile kind of matter, or the action of matter in certain conditions.

Brand's "Encyclopedia of Science" says, "The cause of the phenomena of heat is unknown; but they are supposed to depend upon the presence of a highly attenuated, imponderable, and subtile form of matter, the particles of which repel each other, but are attracted by other bodies." †

That wonder of all wonders,—electricity,— what is it? All nature is running-over full of it, —the earth, the clouds, the metals, our own bodies; yet who can explain it? It is easily produced by rubbing two pieces of matter together, as glass and silk, or a child's hand and a cat's back. See the electric sparks fly! Take this simple fact, now of every-day occurrence. A man stands in New York. He touches the end of a wire, and a man across the ocean in London immediately perceives the fact. He cannot explain how this is done. We say it is done by electricity. Ah! but what is electricity? Is it an immaterial, intangible, conscious spirit from the other world? Three centuries ago it probably would have been explained as such, but now we know it is simply an action of matter, wonderful as it is. It is pro-

* Wells' Natural Philosophy, pp. 293, 207.
† Art,, Heat.

duced from matter; hence it must be either a subtile kind of matter, or the product of matter. Any way, its whole origin is material. It is not an immaterial intelligence. Says Mr. Wells, " Neither do we know whether electricity is a material substance, a property of matter, or the vibration of ether." *

The nature and action of electricity is just as marvelous as that of thought itself. It is no more wonderful or unreasonable that the natural brain should produce thought than that a piece of glass should produce electricity. Every year scientific investigation is revealing new wonders of matter. A man only exposes his ignorance when he says matter cannot do this and cannot do that. He is simply asserting that of which he knows nothing. It is our humble opinion, well founded, we think, too, both in revelation and science, that angels and the celestial beings are as material as men, only that they are more highly organized, more refined,—matter on a higher plane. Who that has carefully observed the wonderful and infinite diversity of matter, even as seen in this earth, will deny the reasonableness of this position? It cannot be disproved, to say the least. When we have found out God to perfection, have entered into his secret laboratory, when we have explored earth, heaven, and hell, and have fathomed all the infinite diversities

* Wells' Natural Philosophy, p. 369

and capabilities of matter, then, and not till then, will it do for us to say what God can do with matter and what he cannot do.

Attraction of gravitation, what is it? It is that power which holds all bodies down to the earth. It pulls the apple off the tree, and causes it to fall to the ground. I hold a stone in my hand. I let it go, and it falls to the ground. Why is this? Because attraction pulls it there. Attraction operates upon all bodies in the universe, however distant. The sun attracts the earth, and holds it in its orbit. Says Wells, "Every portion of matter in the universe attracts every other portion."*

Attraction, then, is either a very subtile kind of matter or else the product of matter. Its source is wholly material. Imagine the tremendous power with which the sun attracts this huge earth. Hitch ten thousand monster ropes and chains to Jupiter, fasten the other end to the earth, and then let the earth drop. How quickly all would be snapped in twain! Yet the sun, by the simple power of attraction, holds this same earth as easily as a boy holds his kite. But can you dissect attraction? Can you cut it and carve it? Can you see it and handle it? Can you hear, smell, or taste it? Can you say it is so long, so wide, and so high? it is black or white, sweet or sour? No; it is just as indefinable and inscru-

* Natural Philosophy, p. 30.

table as thought itself.   Yet no one claims that
it is a living being.   Its root and source is in
matter and of matter.   Till our theologians can
explain some of these wonders of matter, they
need not come to us with their assumptions that
matter cannot think, because we cannot tell how
it thinks.

WHAT IS VEGETABLE AND ANIMAL LIFE ?

Who can explain so simple a thing as vegetable
life, that force by which all vegetables grow?   I
have in my hand a seed.   It is round, hard, and
apparently lifeless.   I can weigh it, measure it,
open and dissect it.   I now take a handful of
common earth, mere particles of dust.   There is
no life here that I can see.   This dust I can weigh,
measure, divide, and analyze.   I put the seed into
it, and add a few drops of water.   The water I
can handle, measure, and analyze.   It is composed of oxygen and hydrogen,—common matter
in its crudest form.   All these elements are nothing but matter.   Now can matter do anything?
Can it stir itself?   Can it move?   Can it arrange
itself in a different manner from that in which
you place it?   Our immaterialist friends say, No,
never; but we say, Yes, when vitalized.

Now look.   Shortly that seed swells out,—becomes larger.   A little sprout begins to put forth,

and tiny roots are thrown out. Particles of that water are taken up, and atoms of matter are appropriated. Day by day a stalk grows up inch by inch, until it stands six feet high and two inches through. Is not all this matter from beginning to end? Is it not all done by matter? Yes. None would be so foolish as to claim that that stalk inclosed an immaterial, intelligent entity, to which this action is due. It is done by the power of vegetable life which the Creator has stored in that little seed, a particle of matter. Ah! there is the secret of it. The principle of life, vegetable life, has been placed there by God. Then inanimate matter can be endowed by the Creator so as to move, and act, and live. Open that green stalk of corn, and you will find that the sap is constantly running up through all its pores. There is life and action; yet it is nothing but matter after all,—matter vitalized. So we see a brain growing larger and stronger and developing thought daily. How and why we don't know any more than why the plant grows. If we assume an immaterial spirit to do the thinking in the brain, we may just as reasonably assume one to do the growing in the plant. But can that stone, that piece of iron, grow? No; God has never bestowed that power upon these, but he has upon other matter, or rather matter in other forms. Is it, then, any harder for God so to organize and endow matter that it will think and reason, than it is to give it vegetable life so that it will grow?

But going a step higher than vegetable life, we have animal life. First we have matter in its crudest form, a mere lifeless mass. The next step higher, as we have seen, is matter in the vegetable form, with vegetable life. The next and third step in matter is when it is organized in the animal. This is seen in the dumb brutes in common with man. Some orders of vegetable life and of animal life are so nearly alike that it is sometimes difficult to mark the dividing line.

But what is animal life? Take that little flea, that fly, that musquito. Each has animal life, is possessed of sensation, of power to do, to move, and to propagate its species. Yet these are nothing but matter organized. No one claims that they have immortal souls. Indeed, believers in the immortality of man's spirit generally agree in denying even intelligence to the higher brutes, much more to the lower.

Now we ask them to tell us what animal life is? It is not reason, it is not intelligence, it is not an immaterial person, an intelligent, thinking being, dwelling in all these fleas, flies, and gnats. No; they say it is simply animal life. Well, then, gross matter can be endowed with life so as to move, eat, drink, propagate, etc. Can these wise spiritualizers put their finger on that animal life and tell us what it is? How long, how wide,

and how deep is it? How much does it weigh?
Can they open and dissect it, can they analyze it
chemically? No; yet they are compelled to acknowledge that it is an attribute which God has
bestowed upon certain organizations of matter.
Simple matter has been endowed by the Creator
with this wonderful faculty.

Now we appeal to any candid man to say
whether this attribute of matter is not just as
mysterious, just as incomprehensible, and just as
difficult to conceive of, as that God should also
organize matter in certain forms so as to be able
to think, reason, and be intelligent. We cannot
tell how matter can think, neither can they tell
us how matter can live, and yet it does both.

HOW DIFFERENT SPECIES OF PLANTS AND ANIMALS ARE PERPETUATED.

Inorganic matter has not the power of produ-
cing a living animal, or even a plant; but at crea-
tion God made the first specimen of all vegetables
and animals, and gave each the power to reproduce
its kind, some one way, some another. Plant a
thousand different seeds in the same soil, and out
of these same material elements each will construct a plant like itself; so each animal begets
another after its own kind. How this can be we
cannot possibly say, yet there is the fact.

I hold in my hand six little seeds. They do
not seem to differ much in size, weight, or color.
They are nothing but matter, at the best. I
place them all side by side in the same soil.
They are moistened by the same dew, warmed
by the same sun, and they grow up together.
But how marvelous! Each little seed has produced a plant quite different from all the rest.
Then look at the various shapes and colors of the
flowers as they open their leaves and blossoms.
One is red, one is white, another is pink, another
violet. Who can explain this mystery? No-
body. Yet this is all the work of mere matter
vitalized by the power of God six thousand years
ago. Look at that apple tree. It bears sour apples. I take a twig from a sweet apple tree, and
graft it into one of the limbs. On that little
twig grow sweet apples, while all around it on
the same tree the apples are sour. The same sap
rises up from the root, and feeds all the limbs
alike; but when it comes to that limb, the same
sap is made into sweet apples instead of sour.
What does this? Is there a mysterious intelligence in that little limb? Oh! no. It is nothing but matter at work, and gross matter at that.
Cannot the God, who can make matter work such
marvels as these, make it think.

Our pleaders for immateriality see such a difference between matter in its higher forms, as
when organized into an angel or the higher classes

of men, and the grosser forms of matter as seen in the lower animals, plants, and minerals, that they conclude these cannot both be material. But we fully believe that the whole difference lies in the quality and superior organization of the matter which the Creator has given one over the other.

Take another simple illustration. Here sits a skillful painter. Before him are his canvas, his brushes, and several kinds of paint,—all nothing but gross matter. They do not look very beautiful in that shape. But now he commences his work. He puts on a little of this paint, a little of that, and some of the other. In due time, lo and behold! there is the figure of an angel. The innocence and loveliness of heaven sit upon it. We cannot admire it too much. Again he takes up the same brushes, with the same paint, and on the same canvas soon is represented the hideous form of a horrid devil. What a contrast in the two pictures! Can they be of the same material? Oh! yes: the only difference is in the way they are put together, or at most, a little tinting of some other paint is added. With the same material he can paint a plant, a beast, or a man. Then cannot God do as much? Yes; we know he does, for we see it every day. Gather up promiscuously a hundred pounds of vegetable matter, a hundred pounds of brute flesh, and as much human flesh, and analyze them all. They will be found to consist largely of the same materials.

Then, reader, it is the organization that makes the plant, the beast, or the man. Yes, sir; and it is the organization that makes the mind, which neither the stone nor the plant possesses.

GOD HAS ORGANIZED MATTER IN CERTAIN FORMS SO THAT IT DOES THINK.

If a false theology had not utterly blinded our eyes to reason and the plainest facts of every-day observation, it would require no argument to prove this proposition. There sits a fly. Is he not material? Is he anything but matter? Will any be foolish enough to claim an immortal soul for him? No: all any one claims is that he has animal life, but no spiritual or immaterial nature. Well, I carefully reach out my hand to put my finger on him. He sees the motion, and, conscious of danger, flies away. Man in danger acts the same as that fly. We know that he reasons in doing so; so does the fly, or else it would not move. I raise my hand to strike that chair, but it does not try to move. Why not, as well as the fly? Because it knows nothing, while the fly understands its danger.

Here is my dog. He thinks. I know he thinks, for I see the fullest evidence of it. I speak to him, and he moves his head, wags his tail, and

comes to me. Could unthinking matter do that?
No. I tell him to do this or that, and he obeys
me. This shows that he knows, that he understands what I say. But our opponents say this
is nothing but instinct; there is no thought,
reason, or intelligence about it. This is sheer
nonsense, for which any reasonable man ought to
blush; but be it so, it only helps our case. For
according to their own position they must admit
that matter can be organized so as to hear, see,
feel, and act. I run a pin into my dog, or I
strike him. See how quickly and keenly he feels
it. He cries out for pain. See his flesh quiver.
There is feeling here: none can deny this. So
our opponents must now admit that matter can
be made to *feel*. There is no possibility of avoid-
ing this conclusion.

But further. My dog can see. Look at his
twinkling eyes. He has as good sight as man
has. Does n't he hear also? How acute his sense
of smelling! You may deny him a mind and
reason, but you cannot deny that he sees, hears,
smells, and feels. Well, he is wholly material, as
we both agree. Then here we have proof which
cannot be evaded in any possible manner that
matter can be organized so as to see, hear, smell,
and feel. This gives us the whole question; for
if God can organize matter to see, to hear, and to
feel, he can as easily organize it to think. Unless
they admit that the dog has an immortal soul,

which they will by no means do, they cannot re-
sort to the favorite evasion which is employed when
we argue that the human eye does see. They re-
ply that it is not the eye that sees, but the immaterial spirit behind it, which sees through the eye
as we see through a telescope. But the dog has
no such immaterial entity back of his eye, yet
he sees; so it must be the material eye that sees
after all.

Take another familiar illustration: Here are a
dozen hen's eggs. I open one, and find nothing
but common matter, largely water with a little
phosphorus, lime, etc. I can see no signs of
thought or even animal life here, nothing which
can see, or hear, or move itself. I put another of
the eggs under a setting hen. In a few days I
behold a living animal breaking out of that shell.
It now has eyes, ears, and can run around, and
feed itself. It can see, hear, and feel. What has
wrought this great difference in the matter which
was in that egg? Has God sent an immortal
soul down to animate it? Oh! no. Simply the
latent animal life in that egg has been developed.
It is just the same matter that it was before, only
it is differently organized. Now that matter can
see and feel.

Let us carry this further. A man is asleep.
Prick his foot with a pin. His foot feels it, and
the nerve immediately carries the impression to
the mind, and the man awakes. In this case it

is the material flesh which feels the pin and informs the mind of it. It is claimed that the immaterial soul is of the same size and shape as the body, and hence it is present in all parts of the body, and that it is after all the soul that feels, and not the flesh? But this theory will not work well for our opponents. According to this view, the immaterial soul of a child can only be the size of a child. Hence it must grow larger as the child grows to man's size. But how can an immaterial thing grow? That which can grow larger must be composed of parts. Hence it can be divided, separated, and thus destroyed, and therefore is not immortal any more than the material body. But to return to that foot. We can positively demonstrate, beyond any contradiction, that in this case it is the material flesh, not the soul at all, which feels the prick of the pin. Here is the proof: Cut off that material leg. Have you cut off the leg of the spirit body which they claim is inside of the material body? Of course they dare not admit that; for if you can cut off the leg of the immaterial body, you could also cut off its head and cut it all up! No, that will not do; so the leg of the spirit body must be there still, hanging out after the material leg of flesh has been amputated! What a predicament that must be for the unfortunate spirit leg!

But the point is, which feels, the material fleshy leg, or the immaterial spirit leg? We will try it.

When the flesh was there, the prick of a pin, the blow of a cane, could be felt. But now that the flesh is gone, thrust in the pin, strike at it and through it with a cane; is there any feeling? Not a particle, as any man will tell you who has lost a limb. So one told me yesterday, when I asked him, and tried the experiment. Then it is not the immaterial body, but the fleshy body, which feels. Take another case. A man's limb is paralyzed. The nerves no longer act. The leg or arm is still alive, but it has no feeling. You may prick it, freeze it, or burn it; but the man feels nothing. I know a person in just this condition. He has frozen all his fingers off because he could not feel when they were cold. What is the difficulty in this case? The material nerve of flesh, the one which feels, is paralyzed and inactive; hence there is no feeling in that limb, though the limb is alive. Now if it is the spirit which feels, and this is present in all the body, why does it not feel as well as before? What can our opponents say to this? Nothing; for it utterly demolishes their immaterial-spirit theory.

But further: we positively know that their pretended spirit-man inside can neither see, hear, smell, taste, nor feel. How do we know this? Put out a man's material eyes, and can he see anything now? No, nothing at all, as any blind man will tell you. So of all the five senses. Destroy the material, physical organs of seeing, hear-

ing, smelling, tasting, or feeling, and the soul can
neither see, hear, smell, taste, nor feel.   This demonstrates that it is the material man which sees,
hears, etc.   If the spirit can see, why does it not
do so?   Why does not the soul of the blind man
see?   Why does not the soul of the deaf man
hear?   Oh! you say, it is cumbered with the flesh.
Then it cannot see through matter, can it?   But
it has been always asserted that the immaterial
spirit is so superior to matter that it can go
through the most solid matter, as through a wall,
through a board, through glass or iron.   But now
this has to be given up, and it is admitted that it
cannot even see, nor hear, nor smell through so
thin a material substance as the human skull!
Poor weak thing! the material ear can do better
than that.   Reader, that boasted immaterial spirit-
man inside is all a fable.   There is no such use-
less tenant there.   God has organized the material, physical man to see, hear, and think; and we
see him in the exercise of this power every day.

    In the case of an amputated limb the person
still feels it to be there for a time.   This is merely
because the mind has so long been accustomed to
having it there that it still seems that it must be
so.   Gradually the brain and nerves become accustomed to the new arrangement, and the sense
of the limb's still being there ceases.

    It is a favorite argument with our opponents
that matter cannot possibly be organized so as to

think and feel. Take as a specimen of all this
reasoning the following from Rev. D. W. Clark,
D. D., Bishop of the M. E. Church, in his book,
" Man All Immortal." He has here stated their
side as forcibly as it can be done. He says:
" We are accustomed to say the eye sees, the ear
hears, the finger feels, and so forth; but such
language is used only in accommodation to our
ignorance, or from the force of habit. It is in-
correct. The eye itself no more sees than the
telescope which we hold before it to assist our
vision; the ear hears not any more than the
trumpet of tin which the deaf man directs toward
the speaker to convey the sound of his voice; and
so with regard to all the organs of sense. They
are but instruments which become the media of
intelligence to the absolute mind, and it uses them
whenever it is inclined or obliged to do so." *

This is the doctrine of the immaterialist. It will
do very well for them to reason that way in the
case of men; but they cannot do it in the case of
the dumb beast, because, as does Bishop Clark in
this very book, they claim that brutes have no
mind, no soul; hence in these cases they are compelled to admit that the dumb animal does see, and
does hear. They have never answered this argument: they never will. They must either admit
that every flea, every musquito, every little gnat,
has an immortal soul, or else they must admit that

* Page 75.

a material animal does see. But if the Almighty can organize matter in a dumb brute so as to see, hear, feel, then can he not do the same in man, and also organize it to reason? But they squarely deny that it is possible for the Almighty to do this.

Hear Bishop Clark's argument upon this point: "The opinion that even *organic matter* could, by *any possibility*, be made to exhibit such power, cannot be received without the most clear and indubitable evidence. What is there to be found in the composition of the brain and nervous system, or in their organization, that would lead us to look for the development of thought, feeling, or conscience in them? The brain has been analyzed, and more than eight-tenths of its substance has been found to be water. Indeed, this, mixed up with a little albumen, a still less quantity of fat, osmazome, phosphorus, acids, salts, and sulphur constitutes its material elements. In all cases, water largely predominates. Take even the *pineal gland*—that interior and mysterious organ of the brain, supposed by Descartes, and by many philosophers after him, to be the peculiar seat of the soul—even this has been analyzed. Its principal elements are found to be phosphate of lime, together with a smaller proportion of carbonate of lime and phosphates of ammonia and magnesia.

"If the brain at large constitutes the soul, then

the soul is only a peculiar combination of oxygen and hydrogen, with albumen, acids, salts, sulphur, etc. Or, if the pineal gland constitutes the soul, then the principal element of soul is phosphate of lime!"*

To immaterialists this may sound like good reasoning; but to us it seems wholly inconclusive. It is simply setting aside the power of God entirely, and arguing that what we cannot do, cannot be done. How foolish!

Try his argument on the organization of dumb beasts. I have in my hand a little live mouse. Behold how bright his eye, how keen his sight. Look at his ear. How sharp his hearing. Prick him with a pin. How quickly he feels it. Again, how acute is his smell. How soon he will find a piece of cheese, or detect the presence of a cat. Here we certainly have sight, hearing, smelling, feeling, and, indeed, all the senses. Let us analyze this little animal as the bishop did the brain, and what do we find? "Eight-tenths of its substance has been found to be water. Indeed, this, mixed up with a little albumen, a still less quantity of fat, osmazome, phosphorus, acids, salts, and sulphur, constitutes its material element. In all cases water largely predominates." We have found simply "a peculiar combination" of oxygen, hydrogen, sulphur, etc.

* Man All Immortal, pp. 57, 58.

How unreasonable to suppose that these gross materials could ever see, hear, or smell! No: it cannot be so. There must be an immaterial, immortal, never-dying soul in that mouse, which did all the seeing and hearing. The mouse must have an immortal soul, and the mosquito surely has a never-dying spirit! Reader, to such absurd conclusions are our opponents driven, to maintain their immaterial theory. It is simply a square denial of the power of God and the common-sense observation of every-day life. Such reasoning is mere appeal to the vulgar prejudices against matter. Let me try it in a different manner.

Here is a fond mother with a dear sweet little girl of four summers, whom she greatly loves: nor can we blame her for being fond of so beautiful a child. The little girl has bright, twinkling eyes, plump, rosy cheeks, curly hair, finely shaped, dimpled hands, and a fair complexion. She is neatly dressed in the most tasteful manner. How the mother loves to throw her arms around her, and press her to her heart! But stop. Let us put this lovely object into the chemical laboratory, and analyze it. A thorough analysis shows that four-fifths of that body is nothing but water, a few parts albumen, sulphur, phosphorus, salts, acids, and a little fatty matter. Lay them out here each by itself. Is there anything very lovely here? Would you like to embrace and kiss these? Oh, no; the loveliness is all gone. And yet but a

few minutes ago, that mother was caressing these
very elements in the most affectionate manner.
Was she then so much in love with a little water,
phosphorus, and sulphur? How ridiculous this
seems to be! It is no more absurd, however, than
the arguments of our opponents,—that a little
water, sulphur, etc., cannot think.

THE BEAUTY AND POWER OF MATTER LIES IN ITS ORGANIZATION.

But the falsity of this kind of reasoning lies
just in this: It takes the unorganized, unvitalized
elements separately, and reasons as to what these
can do, and what these can be, and what they
cannot do in this condition. It sets aside the
very points at issue; namely, organization and
proper combination. It is just like taking an
exquisite painting, and undertaking to prove that
there is nothing beautiful about it by the same
process. Put that painting into the chemical
laboratory, wash off the paint with an acid, analyze its elements; and what do you find? A
little oil, a few ounces of lead, and several different minerals. Lay them out there side by side.
Now I can sneeringly say, Where is its beauty?
Where its comely form? Where is there anything to be admired? But how absurd would
be such a course? The whole beauty of that

picture is, not in the rough material, but in their skillful combination and arrangement. Destroy the combination, and the beauty is gone, the picture is destroyed.

Just so foolish does he reason who undertakes to analyze a man's brain, and finding only water, phosphorus, albumen, etc., sneeringly says, "This cannot reason, this cannot think." No, very true; in that shape they cannot. But as God put them together, they can think, and they do. Further than this, we know that a man's brain does think; because in more than one case it has been seen in the act of thinking. A certain man had by an injury a large piece entirely removed from the top of his skull. It exposed two or three square inches of his brain, but did not kill him. Interesting observations were made in his case by physicians. When he was asleep, the brain would settle down, and become greatly contracted. It would be all quiet. The moment he awoke, the brain would grow larger and begin to quiver. As he entered into conversation, this motion of the brain increased. When his mind became agitated, this motion was very rapid.

What does this show? It shows that the brain does think. The science of phrenology confirms the fact that the brain does think. It shows that the size and quality of a man's brain determine the capacity of his mind. A large brain, of a fine organization, always gives a giant mind.

Even Bishop Clark thus inadvertantly admits this fact: "A finer and more perfect organization in the human species affords finer development of mental power." *   Look at the charts and busts exhibited by the phrenologist. It will be seen that the organization of the brain has been the measure of the mental man.

"The average Hottentot is inferior in intellectual capacity to the average European; and this is not because an inferior kind of soul has taken up its abode in the Hottentot's tenament of clay, but because his physical organization is less perfect. Among the lower animals, mental power is manifested in proportion to the size and quality of the brain; thus the superior sagacity of the monkey, the dog, the horse, and the elephant is owing to the possession of superior cerebral organization. 'The size of the brain,' says Dr. Gray, 'appears to bear a general relation to the intellectual capacity of the individual. Cuvier's weighed rather more than 64 ounces, that of the late Dr. Abercrombie 63 ounces, and that of Dupuytren 62½ ounces. On the other hand, the brain of the idiot seldom weighs more than 23 ounces.' "†

It is not the mere size of the brain that is the measure of mental power, but the fineness of the material and the way it is organized, must be considered. Hence it is that a practiced phrenolo-

* Man All Immortal p. 99.
† Immortality, p. 75, by J. H. Whitmore.

gist can read a man's character by simply feeling
of his head. What is insanity? Generally the
wildest ravings result from some derangement of
the brain, a nervous disease, a fracture of the skull,
or a derangement of the fluids in the system. Cure
the nervous disease, restore the fractured skull to
its position, and thus put it in order again, and
the mental disorder at once ceases. But if the
mind is immortal and indestructible, how can it
ever become insane? How can it become diseased?

Another fact proves that the mind results from
the physical organization; namely, that the mind
grows with the growth of the body, and decays
with its decay. Hence, who expects to find a
man's intellect in the body of a babe or of a child?
Paul truly says, "When I was a child, I spake as
a child, I understood as a child, I thought as a
child." 1 Cor. 13:12. As the brain grows up to
maturity, the mind also developes; and then in
old age, as the body grows weak, the mind grows
weak also, till you have second childhood, so familiar to everybody. This should not be so, if the
mind of man is immaterial and separate from the
physical man. But it is objected that in some
cases the body is weak and sickly while the mind
is vigorous and powerful; that sometimes the mind
retains its full faculties, even to the last breath.
But this is a very weak objection, easily answered. Cases like these are rare; they are the
exception. All parts of the body are not always

affected alike by health or by sickness.   That is, a man may be dying of the consumption, his lungs nearly consumed; and yet his heart may be sound and healthy, his eye bright and keen, his ear sharp to hear.   Or a man's eye may be very weak, but his hearing acute; his liver may be wholly diseased, and his lungs may be sound. A man may be sick in any one part of his body, and well and strong in another.   Hence the cases mentioned simply show that while other parts of the body are feeble, the brain is sound and healthy.   But the general rule, the world over, is, " A sound mind in a sound body."

A further fact to be noticed is that the mind, the intellect, can be developed and enlarged by exercise and training, the same as any other part of the system.   See that awkward, clumsy-fingered young man learning to write.   What great awkward scratches he makes!   What is the matter?   His fingers have not been disciplined. They have not learned how to hold and guide the pen with ease.   But after long training he can execute the finest penmanship with great precision.   Or take it in a more physical sense.   A strong young man undertakes to lift a heavy weight for the first time.   He finds it very difficult.   He cannot lift much; but he keeps practicing, training his muscles, till by and by he can lift several times as much as in the beginning. His muscles have grown stronger by exercise.

Just so with the mind. An undisciplined, unexercised mind is very weak intellectually; but close application and continued training develop strong, vigorous powers of thinking. All these facts show that the intellect is wholly dependent upon the physical organization, the same as any other power of a man.

If a child should be born into the world, and grow up without ever having the use of any of his five senses, viz., hearing, seeing, smelling, tasting or feeling, he could never have any thought, for he would have nothing about which to think. A babe's mind is a perfect blank. It knows nothing. Every idea it afterward has, it must learn from what it hears, sees, feels, tastes, or smells. This clearly demonstrates that mind, thought, and intelligence come from without, from the material world; and not from within, from the spirit world.

CAUSE AND EFFECT CONFOUNDED.

Those who deny that matter can be so organized as to think, love, hope, fear, etc., have contrasted this action or attribute of organized matter with matter itself; and because the distinctive characteristics of matter, such as size, form, weight, etc., are not applicable to these qualities, they have fallen into the inexcusable error of assuming that there must be an immaterial spirit to produce

thought, love, hope, etc. They ask, Is love round
or square? Is fear triangular or hexagonal? Is
hope long or short? How much does anger
weigh? Thus they entirely ignore the difference
between matter and its operations. It is hard to
credit that learned men should make such blun-
ders, yet it is a fact. Thus Joseph Cook reasons:
" When Cæsar saw Brutus stab, and muffled up
his face at the foot of Pompey's statue, was his
grief round or square, or triangular. [Laughter.]
When Lincoln, by a stroke of his pen, manumitted
four million slaves, was his choice hexagonal or
octagonal? "   " These questions show that the
terms which we apply to *matter* are totally
inapplicable and meaningless when applied to
mind." *

This superficial reasoning would prove that not
only beasts, but even vegetables, have immortal
souls. The dog is angry, the ox hopes for his
dinner, and the cat loves her kitten. Try the
same reasoning on the sweetness of sugar, the
sourness of a lemon, the elasticity of rubber, and
the density of iron. Is sweetness round, or sourness square, or elasticity crooked, or density
triangular? [Laughter.] Then these intangible qualities must be proof of an immaterial
spirit in sugar, lemon, rubber, and iron, the same
as intangible thought proves an immaterial spirit
in man! What nonsense! As it is utterly impos-

* Lecture on Biology, p. 224.

sible for sweetness or sourness, elasticity or density, to exist separate and apart from the material substances which give rise to these qualities, so it is just as impossible for mind to exist separate from the brain which produces it. Just try to imagine pure thought wholly separate and apart from any organized being! How would you describe it? Nay; how would you even conceive of it? You could as well conceive of motion without a moving body, or sweetness as an abstract thing without any material substance to produce it. It is astonishing how a false theory will blind the wisest men.

But it is said with much show of reason, If intelligence is the result of organization, then organization must precede intelligence. Who then organized the first intelligent being? This is simply the old and always recurring question as to the origin of the Creator himself. It is a question which no theory of existence has ever been able to answer. It is no more difficult for us with our view than for our opponents with their view, for neither the one nor the other can answer it at all. It is infinitely beyond all human reasoning. The eternal pre-existence of God is assumed, and has to be assumed by all believers in a Supreme Being. The *how* and *why* of this incomprehensible existence none pretend to know or even guess.

The assumption that God is a pure, immaterial spirit does not relieve the difficulty any; for even such an immaterial spirit essence, if there could be such a thing, must be organized into a person, or else it would be only a mere indefinite essence but no person at all. But the God of the Bible is a person, a real being, dwelling in a definite place, sitting upon a throne, etc. Furthermore, those who claim that God is an immaterial spirit, claim just the same for angels. But are not angels organized, personal beings? Did not God create them? To say that they are not organized beings is to claim that they are eternal, uncreated, self-existent, and equal to God himself! So even a spirit being must be organized. Hence, in assuming that God, is immaterial, the difficulty is only shifted, and moved a little farther off, but not solved after all. In either case it must be admitted that organization must precede thought whatever be the nature of his essence.

INSTINCT AND REASON.

Our opponents are constantly decrying matter, and attributing all excellence to immateriality. But an examination of nature shows that the Creator has used this same matter to bring about the infinite diversity which is seen everywhere, from the grain of sand up to the highest in-

telligence. First we have matter in its coarsest
and crudest condition,—mineral matter, unorganized matter, such as a handful of dust, a piece of
granite, a wedge of gold. Next higher we have
organized and vitalized matter in the vegetable
kingdom. Going still higher, we have the same
matter more highly organized in the animal
kingdom.

I have in my hand a school book, "The Philosophy of Natural History," by John Ware, M.
D. He has clearly stated many points bearing
upon this question. He says:—

"We have the most complete specimen of what
instinct alone can do in such insects as the ant,
bee, wasp, and spider; and of what intelligence
can do in such animals as the horse, dog, beaver,
and elephant, and more than all, in man. Instinct
probably predominates in all the animals below
man, and the presence of a true intelligence is not
directly detected below the vertebral animals, except among the higher species of the articulata
and mollusca. Its influence becomes more marked
as we ascend through fishes, reptiles, and birds to
the mammalia; but it is only among the most
elevated of the last that it assumes an important
rank as a directing power, and it is never a pre-
dominant one except in man.

"Man thus stands on an eminence high above
all other animals; and yet so far as we are able to
analyze their character, their faculties are not

specifically distinct from his, but appear to differ from them rather in degree than in kind. Animals exhibit the same sentiments, the same affections, the same emotions, the same passions as man. Their lives are governed by certain motives, and are directed to certain objects in common with his."*

I believe that this author has candidly stated the truth in the preceding extract. We simply have an ascending gradation in the different forms of matter,—mineral, vegetable, and animal, lower and higher.

Here I might give innumerable examples of clearly defined reason, intelligence, or mind in the lower animals. But waiving all this, we will grant just what our opponents claim, namely, that the dumb beasts never reason nor think, that they are wholly guided by instinct. Instinct moves them to eat, to drink, to open their eyes, to listen with their ears, to smell, to feel, to flee from danger, and to do a thousand things which we observe daily. This is all done by instinct, and the beast is merely organized matter, and nothing else. Now see what follows from this,—the Creator has so vitalized, so organized this matter that it can see and hear, can eat and drink, can rise up and lie down, can defend itself, can come at a call, or go at a command, can work, build houses, and do a thousand things. Even Bishop Clark,

*Page 405.

writing against our position, makes the following wonderful admission:—

"In fact, surveying the whole ground, we can hardly wonder at the enthusiasm with which a modern writer, quoted by Mr. Brodie, kindles up: 'There is,' says he, 'hardly a mechanical pursuit in which insects do not excel. They are excellent weavers, house-builders, architects; they make diving-bells, bore galleries, raise vaults, construct bridges; they line their houses with tapestry, clean them, ventilate them, and close them with admirably-fitted swing-doors; they build and store warehouses, construct traps in the greatest variety, hunt skillfully, rob and plunder; they poison, saber, and strangle their enemies; they have social laws, a common language, division of labor, and gradations of rank; they maintain armies, go to war, send out scouts, appoint sentinels, carry off prisoners, keep slaves, and tend domestic animals. In short, they are a miniature copy of men rather than of the inferior vertebrata.' This description is highly wrought, but not so highly but that its substantial basis in fact will be readily recognized."*

Reader, all this is done by mere matter! So the bishop argues; so our opponents believe. Now if the blessed God can vitalize and organize matter so as to do all these wonderful things, can he not just as easily go a little farther and organize

* Man All Immortal, p. 95.

matter so as to think, be intelligent, and reason?
We believe the conclusion is legitimate, and that
facts in connection with the human mind show it
is the truth.   God has organized a material brain
which does think and reason.

FROM WHENCE COMES THE IMMORTAL SPIRIT?

We now have a few questions for our opponents to answer.   If man has an immortal, immaterial, deathless spirit, we ask, From whence does
it come? and how is it propagated?   Was it conscious in a pre-existent state, in some other world,
and from thence is sent into the human body at
birth?   Or is soul created by the Lord at the
birth of every child?   Or is it begotten, like the
body, and perpetuated with the body?   One of
these three positions must be taken.   Indeed, our
opponents have always taken some one of these
positions, though they are not all agreed which
one to adopt.   Shall we advocate the pre-existence of the soul, that it lived in some other world
before it came into the body?   If so, why do we
not remember having living somewhere else?
Strange that we should have so utterly forgotten
all the past.   Then, why does not the soul come
into the body pure and sinless, inclined to holiness?
How does it happen, moreover, that children are so

much like their parents, in their souls as well as in
their bodies, mentally as well as physically? But
as none except the Mormons now hold to the
foolish idea of pre-existence, we will let it pass.

Shall we say, then, that souls are created in
heaven and sent into each body at birth? This
theory would involve a greater difficulty than the
other. The Lord must be continually creating,
every minute, additional immortal souls. More
than that, this would make him sanction prostitu-
tion and adultery. A child is begotten in adultery,
in the most wicked and corrupt manner. Must
God immediately create a soul for that child?
This would make God a party to sin. Moreover,
if God thus creates immaterial souls, he must
either make them pure and holy, or impure and
sinful. The latter supposition is inconsistent with
the character of God; and if the former be the
true one, how shall we account for the natural
depravity of the human soul? The evidence of
our eyes proves that children are born predisposed
to sin, some of them much more so than others.
According to this theory a father is not the father
of the soul of his child, for that was created in the
other world. But how does it happen, then, that
children are generally so much like their parents,
mentally as well as physically? In fact, this immortal-soul theory breaks down everywhere you
touch it.

Then, again, if the soul is thus created a separate entity, an intelligent being before it is placed in the body, why do we not remember even that little time that we existed before we were in the body? And again, at what time is the soul sent into the body, and what is its condition before it is placed there? Is it just at birth, or a little after, or some time before? Does it come fully grown? or is it a baby soul that grows up afterward? If so, what makes it grow? On what does it feed? Does it grow out of the material which the body eats? Then it must be material itself. No: that wont do. Well, is it placed in the body fully grown—man's size? How, then, can it be cramped up in so small a space? And why does not the soul of a baby reason and think like a man's, if it is a man's?

If the soul is not pre-existent, neither created directly at birth, it must be propagated with the body. Indeed, this theory has been held by many. Says Dr. Knapp, "The reason why this theory is so much preferred by theologians, is that it affords the easiest solution of the doctrine of native depravity."* But the moment you adopt this theory you come upon our ground, and admit that the soul is material. For how could an immaterial soul beget another immaterial soul? Are these intangible souls male and female? and can they beget children? The very idea is utterly

* Knapp's Christian Theology, p. 202.

absurd and untenable. No. If souls are begotten, then they must be material. This is what
all admit who hold this theory. Thus Dr. Knapp
says:—

"This hypothesis is not, however, free from ob-
jections; and it is very difficult to reconcile it
with some philosophical opinions which are uni-
versally received. We cannot, for example, easily conceive how generation and propagation can
take place without extension. But we cannot
predicate extension of the soul without making it
a material substance. Tertullian and others of
the Fathers affirm, indeed, that the soul of man,
and that *spirit* in general, is not perfectly pure
and simple, but of a refined, material nature, of
which, consequently, *extension* may be predica-
ted." *

But is this true that souls beget souls? and are
spirits male and female? If they are material,
and are begotten with the body, then the pre-
sumption is that they will also die with it. How
much more natural and consistent is the simple
truth, that man is a unit, that his mental powers
grow out of his physical organization. A father
begets a child of his own person; hence that child
naturally partakes of the peculiarities of his father, both physical and mental. This we everywhere see to be the case. "Like father, like
son." This accounts for our fallen natures, and

* Christian Theology, p. 202.

inherited weaknesses of body and mind. The mental likeness of children to their parents is generally just as great as their physical likeness, and often even greater. With our view of man, this is just what we should expect; but on the supposition that the soul is an immaterial entity sent down directly from God, it is wholly inexplicable.

THE DISEMBODIED SPIRIT.

It is claimed by the believers in the immateriality of the soul that the disembodied spirit is "an entity" or a "principle," immaterial and without any organism. If the spirit is not an organized material body, then it has no head, no hands, no feet, no eyes, no ears, no tongue, and no brain. But how can a soul sing without a tongue, think without a brain, see without eyes, walk without feet, feel without nerves, and love without a heart? It is strange beyond explanation that a sane man should ever have conceived of such "an entity." A queer kind of a world that spirit land must be! According to this theory as soon as the soul leaves the body it becomes deaf, blind, dumb, and idiotic, since it lacks every organ by which to gain an idea or to express one!

What must be the shape of this immaterial spirit? As it has neither arms, legs, head, nor heart, is it a body? If so, what is its shape? Is it round, flat, square, oblong, or three cornered? But probably it has no shape, for if it has shape it must be material.

What then is the *size* of the spirit? Is it as large as a horse or as small as a flea? But *size* is a property of matter, and therefore the spirit has no size at all. It is neither big nor little. What nonsense! a real man, and yet have neither form, size, shape, body, head, hands, nor feet!

MATERIAL AND IMMATERIAL.

It is the weakest nonsense to talk about material and "immaterial substances." There are no reasons for making such a distinction. The heaviest metal can be converted into gas many times lighter than the air. Beginning with the heaviest known substance, platinum, we have a regular gradation up through the metals, wood, flesh, water, air, gas, odor, magnetism, electricity, gravitation, heat, and light—all material substances as must be admitted. But are not light, heat, magnetism, electricity, and air sufficiently attenuated and powerful to meet the popular ideas of an "immaterial substance?" Certainly, and yet these are all either material substances or the action of matter.

Magnetism is one of the most wonderful forces in nature. The magnetic rays will pass through solid wood, glass, or even platinum, and seize a bar of iron and move it around rapidly. You can see nothing, yet it must be material as the result shows. The air when at rest is unrecognizable by any of the senses. It can neither be seen, heard, felt, tasted, nor smelled; and even when in motion we only recognize it by its pressure on our bodies. It might almost seem to justify the term, "an immaterial thing." And yet this same air is as material as a stone or a tree. It is composed of $\frac{1}{5}$ oxygen and $\frac{4}{5}$ nitrogen. It can be analyzed, weighed, and measured. It has an actual weight of fifteen pounds to the square inch upon all bodies at the level of the sea. It has been reduced by extreme cold and immense pressure into a liquid substance of the density of water.

Any substance we see around us, as a piece of flesh, a garment of cloth, a stick of wood, a stone, or a silver dollar, can be converted into an invisible gas, and yet not a particle of the matter be destroyed. It is inconceivable how infinitely small are the ultimate atoms of which all matter is composed. "A grain of musk has been kept freely exposed to the air of a room of which the door and windows were constantly kept open, for a period of two years, and during all this time the air, though constantly changed, was densely impregnated with the odor of musk, and yet at the end of that time the particle was found not to have greatly diminished in weight. During all this period every particle of the atmosphere which produced the sense of odor must have contained a certain quantity of musk." *

It is a fact worth noticing that from matter in an invisible condition come the most powerful agents in nature, such as steam, compressed air, heat, electricity, etc. It is not at all incredible, then, that God should create the higher order of beings, such as angels, out of matter in an invisible state; yet they would be material all the same.

In a drop of water there are thousands of living, moving animals, each one perfect in its way, full of life and activity. And though they are wholly invisible to the unaided eye, yet they are as material as the water itself. With such facts before us, it is not best to hastily conclude that whatever phenomenon in nature we cannot readily comprehend, cannot weigh, measure, and analyze, must be produced by immaterial spirits. Ignorance, not knowledge, is the source of this unphilosophical notion of an immaterial entity. It is a relic of the superstition handed down from heathenism and the Dark Ages.

Moreover, we would ask these wise men who are so positive as to what matter can do and what it cannot do, how it is that the immaterial, intangible essence which has not one particle of materiality about it, which can in no wise be grasped, nor held, nor handled by material or-

* Wells' Natural Philosophy, p. 13.

gans,—we ask how this immaterial soul can come
in contact with a physical body any way? What
point of contact can there possibly be between
such a thing and the material brain? How can
it operate upon our organs of hearing, smelling,
or tasting? In fact, how can it be so closely con-
fined in this material form? Why can't it leave
the body at will? But it cannot. If there is
such a soul inside, we know that the body holds
it with a death-like grasp; and however much
the soul may desire to flee, it cannot possibly get
away till the material body is dead, and has lost
all its strength and power to hold even a straw.
These difficulties, to our mind, are tenfold greater
than those attending the admission of the simple
truth that the material brain has been so organized as to think.

The advocates of the immortal-soul theory
freely admit that they cannot explain how the
soul can act upon a material brain. Indeed, they
admit that they cannot tell what the soul is.
Bishop Clark himself thus speaks: "We confess
that we know not in what the *essence* of soul,
or spirit, consists. We readily acknowledge our
ignorance of the *essence*, the *subject-being*, of
matter. We make the same confession—and under the same limitations—concerning the soul."*
Another doctor of divinity says, "We do not un-

* Man All Immortal, p. 29.

derstand the true nature of spirit, and cannot therefore determine what is or is not possible respecting it." *

How do they know, then, but that the soul is material after all? They do not know; and after they have argued and philosophized to the end of the subject, one confession like the above overturns all their speculations. They are arguing about something of which they know nothing.

If the soul is a living, intelligent entity, capable of thinking, moving about, and acting as well out of the body as in it, we ask, What was the use of making the body for it any way? Why not leave it without the clog of this poor, gross, material body? Indeed, if our immaterialist friends are right, it would have been a great blessing to the spirit to have left it without the body; for they are always telling how the flesh weighs down the immortal spirit, and clogs its movements, and with what speed the disembodied spirit will travel when freed from the body, with what power it will then act. Then why do we have the body at all? Let those answer who can.

* Knapp's Christian Theology, p. 202.

CAUSE OF INFIDELITY AMONG SCIENTISTS.

The intelligent reader is aware that modern scientific men are, to a great extent, becoming skeptical. I am fully satisfied that one great cause of this skepticism is found in the false view which theologians have held concerning mind and matter. Scientific men readily see that, given the first organization of each species to begin with, and all the phenomena of nature, vegetable, animal, and mental, can be readily accounted for in the physical organization. Hence physicians, physiologists, and phrenologists in particular, have been largely inclined to materialism. Says Dr. Knapp, speaking of the view that the soul is material, "It has always been the favorite theory of psychologists and physicians."* Seeing the absurdity of the doctrine of immateriality and natural immortality, they have given up their old theology, and thrown away their religion with it. Had they been taught the true doctrine of mind and intelligence, it would have done much to save them from their skepticism.

* Christian Theology, p. 202.

IS MATTER NATURALLY CORRUPT ?

These immaterialists are always asserting how mean, corrupt, polluted, weak, and every way inferior, matter is. To hear them talk, you would suppose that matter must be very hateful to God. But if matter is naturally so corrupt and mean, why has God created so much of it? Who made of matter all those numberless millions of worlds on high? Every astronomer knows that they are all as material as our own earth. Ghosts do not cast shadows, but the moon and other heavenly bodies do. Who made the moon? Who made the earth? the air? the water? the dust? the rocks? the plants? the trees? the insects? the animals? and our material bodies? God made them all of matter; yea, and pronounced them "very good." Gen. 1 : 31. To these very things God always appeals as the highest proof of his power, glory, and Godhead. "The heavens declare the glory of God; and the firmament showeth his handiwork." Ps. 19 : 1. Again: " He hath made the earth by his power, he hath established the world by his wisdom, and hath stretched out the heavens by his discretion." Jer. 10 : 12. To the idolatrous Athenians he is introduced as the "God that made the world, and all things therein." Acts 17 : 24. Paul declares that "by the things

that are made, his eternal power and Godhead"
are clearly seen. Rom. 1: 20. When the Lord
would convince Job of his might and greatness,
he pointed to the foundations of the earth, which
he had laid (Job 38 : 1–6), to the sea (verse 8), to
the clouds (verse 9), to the stars (verses 31–33),
to the lightnings (verse 35), to the lions (verse 39),
and to all of the beasts of the earth which he had
made (Chap. 39). All these are material, made
of the dust of the ground. God is not ashamed
to appeal to these material things as the highest
proof of his glory.

Is it true, then, that the matter which God has
made is so corrupt and naturally sinful as immaterialists claim? Then God would be the author
of sin. God made man of the dust of the ground.
Gen. 2 : 7. God made the beautiful and holy
Eden of matter, of the ground. Yea; even the
tree of life itself grew out of the ground. Gen.
2 : 8–15. God's divine Son, who came to redeem
men, was a material being. He was born of a
woman, had flesh and bones, walked upon our
earth, ate its material food, breathed its material
air, and drank its material water.

"It is not wise to repudiate materialism till we
see what connection it has with our final salvation.
And here we inquire, How are we to be saved?
From our opposers, as well as from the Bible,
comes the answer, By the *death* of Christ. Very
well. Then could we be saved without his death?

All agree we could not.   This paves the way for
another important question, If we are saved by
the *death* of Christ, and could not be saved without his death, are we saved by the death of a *material* Christ?   or by the death of an immaterial
Christ?   Own the truth, let the result be what it
may.   Did an immaterial Christ die for us?   You
say No.   Then was it not a *material* Christ that
died?   Certainly.   So you admit that a material
Christ died to save us, and that otherwise salvation would not have been possible, thus predicat-
ing your hope of salvation upon the death of
materiality.   No matter whether there was an
immaterial entity within him or not, so long as
that did not die; and we expressly read, "Christ
died for us," and "We are reconciled to God by
the death of his Son;" so we are indebted for salvation to the death of that part of Christ which
could and did die, even if he had forty entities
that could not and did not die; and the part that
died for our sins was *material.*   Hear it, ye hat-
ers of materialism!   The foundation-stone of the
system of salvation, from your own showing, is
materiality, and there is no escape from the conclusion." *

Then in the resurrection, our material bodies
are to be saved and immortalized.   1 Cor. 15:
51–55.   Yes, and finally, this material earth is to

* *Bible Banner.*

be purified from the curse, and made the eternal home of the saints.   Rev. 21 : 1–5.

But here I leave this very interesting question, having only glanced at a few of the innumerable proofs in favor of the materiality of all things.   I have endeavored to avoid the fine metaphysical arguments which are generally employed on this topic, and use only those common facts of every-day observation with which every child is familiar.

www.ingramcontent.com/pod-product-compliance
Lightning Source LLC
Chambersburg PA
CBHW021523090426
42739CB00007B/757